Original title:
Painted Peace

Copyright © 2024 Creative Arts Management OÜ
All rights reserved.

Author: Victor Mercer
ISBN HARDBACK: 978-9916-90-702-3
ISBN PAPERBACK: 978-9916-90-703-0

Chromatic Comfort

In hues that dance and blend so bright,
A canvas glows with pure delight.
Colors whisper soft and low,
Embracing hearts where calm can flow.

Essence of Equanimity

In stillness lies a gentle truth,
A balanced heart, a soul uncouth.
Like water smooth beneath the sun,
Equanimity, our hearts have won.

Serenity in Strokes

With every brush, a story wakes,
A tranquil song that softly breaks.
In flowing lines, our spirit sings,
Serenity in what art brings.

Calming Canvases

A tapestry of soft embrace,
In every shade, a tranquil space.
Where dreams can drift and worries cease,
Calming canvases, our peace increase.

Colors Wrapped in Silence

Whispers of hues in the night,
Soft shadows dance out of sight,
Crimson and gold intertwine,
A palette lost, sweet and divine.

Gentle breezes carry a song,
In stillness, the colors belong,
Cerulean dreams take their flight,
Wrapped in the quilt of the night.

Reflections of Calm Waters

Stillness rests upon the lake,
Mirrored skies, the clouds awake,
Ripples weave a whispered tale,
Nestled beneath the twilight veil.

Silhouettes of trees in line,
Embraced by waters, so divine,
Each reflection tells a story,
In the silence, find the glory.

The Gentle Touch of Twilight

As daylight fades, the stars ignite,
A tender kiss from day to night,
Soft pastels drift through the air,
In twilight's arms, there's nothing to bear.

Whispers of dusk, a calming peace,
Where worries fade and tensions cease,
Eyes close softly, dreams take flight,
Embraced within the gentle night.

Vivid Veils of Serenity

In gardens where the wildflowers bloom,
Colors bright dispel the gloom,
Nature's brush, it sweeps away,
An artist's heart in full display.

Gossamer dreams in the evening light,
Dance on petals, pure delight,
Each bloom a sigh, so soft and sweet,
Where serenity and joy meet.

Hues of Happiness

In the morning light, smiles bloom,
Golden rays dispel the gloom.
Joy dances in every hue,
Painting the world anew.

Laughter echoes through the air,
Brightening hearts everywhere.
Like flowers swaying in the breeze,
Happiness flows with such ease.

Children play, their spirits free,
Chasing dreams, just let them be.
Every moment filled with cheer,
A symphony we hold dear.

In every corner, love resides,
Together we face the tides.
With colors of joy, we stand tall,
In hues of happiness, we fall.

Dreamlike Colorfields

In realms of dreams, colors blend,
A canvas where soft whispers send.
Gently flowing, a radiant stream,
Awakening our deepest dream.

Soft pastels in twilight's embrace,
Paint the sky with delicate grace.
Each stroke a tender lullaby,
Inviting the stars to sigh.

Velvet nights, under moon's glow,
Create spaces where visions flow.
Chromatic wonders softly gleam,
In this world of boundless dream.

A swirl of colors, hearts ignite,
Guiding lost souls through the night.
In dreamlike fields, we find our home,
A place where our spirits roam.

Tranquility's Brush

In the morning's gentle light,
Whispers of the dawn arise,
Color spills from nature's hands,
Painting peace across the skies.

Trees sway softly in the breeze,
Leaves dance with a quiet grace,
Clouds drift lazily above,
In this calm, we find our place.

A Whisper of Hues

Pastel skies at sunset glow,
Orange, pink, and lavender,
Each shade tells a silent tale,
In the fading light, we stir.

Rippling waters catch the hues,
Reflecting dreams that gently drift,
In this moment, colors blend,
Nature's soft and precious gift.

Evocations of Stillness

The world slows in twilight's hand,
Stars awaken, one by one,
Silent shadows stretch and yawn,
In the night, all is undone.

Crickets sing a lullaby,
Moonlit paths invite us near,
Deep within this quiet space,
We embrace what we hold dear.

Chroma and Calm

Vibrant gardens bloom anew,
Life in every shade and tone,
Petals whisper sweet secrets,
In their beauty, we are home.

The breeze carries fragrance soft,
Each scent a memory traced,
In this tapestry of life,
Chroma and calm interlaced.

The Palette of Silence

In the quiet dusk, shadows play,
Whispers of night brush the day.
Colors blend in muted shades,
Softly woven, the silence fades.

Stars emerge, a jeweled sky,
Breezes hum a gentle sigh.
Each breath of night, a soft embrace,
Cradling dreams in endless space.

Delicate Dosing of Peace

Morning light breaks, so tender,
Birds sing notes, a calming splendor.
Each drop of dew, a soothing balm,
Nature's symphony, pure and calm.

Petals open, colors dance,
In the breeze, the trees prance.
With every moment, peace entwines,
In simple joys, our spirit shines.

Peaceful Palettes

Canvas stretched, hues entwine,
Gentle strokes, a design divine.
Soft greens swirl with skies of blue,
In artful whispers, dreams come true.

Each splash of color tells a tale,
A journey through calm, where hearts sail.
Crafting solace in every hue,
In peaceful palettes, we renew.

The Art of Calm

Brush in hand, the stillness flows,
Each stroke calms, as the spirit knows.
Lines that linger, shadows that rest,
In artful silence, we find our quest.

A tranquil heart, a peaceful mind,
In every creation, serenity finds.
The canvas whispers, soft and low,
Within its depths, true calm will grow.

Hues of Harmony

In the dawn's soft, golden light,
Colors blend with pure delight,
Whispers of the day arise,
Nature's song beneath the skies.

Fields of green and skies of blue,
Paint a picture, calm and true,
Every shade, a note in tune,
Harmonies that make us swoon.

Strokes of Tranquility

Gentle waves on quiet shores,
Calm surrounds, my spirit soars,
Brush the canvas, fresh and bright,
Every stroke, a touch of light.

In the silence, moments blend,
Every shadow, every bend,
Softly painted, emotions flow,
Tranquil thoughts begin to grow.

The Art of Stillness

In stillness lies a secret grace,
A moment's pause, a warm embrace,
Breathe in deep the earth's sweet scent,
Find the peace in what is meant.

In the quiet, dreams take flight,
Stars above, a guiding light,
Crafting stories, softly told,
The art of stillness, pure as gold.

Brushstrokes of Bliss

With every brushstroke, joy unfolds,
A tapestry of colors bold,
Dancing hues in joyful play,
Capture bliss in each new day.

Every canvas, fresh and bright,
Whispers secrets, pure delight,
In this world of vibrant grace,
Find your heart's most perfect place.

Explorations in Stillness

In the hush of dawn's warm glow,
A whisper of peace begins to flow.
Nature breathes with gentle grace,
Time pauses in this sacred space.

Leaves rustle soft, a subtle sound,
As shadows shift upon the ground.
Finding calm within the storm,
In stillness, a new self is born.

Mountains stand with silent pride,
Holding secrets deep inside.
The world unfolds, a canvas vast,
In stillness, we find our path at last.

Every moment holds a chance,
To embrace the quiet dance.
With each breath, our spirits rise,
In stillness, we find the skies.

The Quiet Canvas

A blank slate waits, inviting dreams,
Where silence speaks in vibrant seams.
With gentle strokes, the heart releases,
The artist's mind, a dance of pieces.

Colors blend in soft embrace,
Whispers of life fill empty space.
Each hue a story yet untold,
Crafting visions, both brave and bold.

Through quiet moments, visions grow,
As skills and passions softly flow.
In every layer, a truth revealed,
On this canvas, hearts are healed.

In the stillness, brush meets paint,
Transforming thoughts, both wild and quaint.
The quiet canvas, pure and free,
A world of wonder waits for me.

Echoes in Acrylic

Acrylic flows in vibrant streams,
Creating worlds that spark our dreams.
Each color sings with tales of old,
Echoes of life in shades of bold.

Brush in hand, I seek to find,
The rhythm of the heart and mind.
With every stroke, the past awakes,
In echoes, a new spirit takes.

Layers build like stories told,
Each whispering secret, rich and gold.
With echoes lingering in each hue,
The canvas breathes, alive and true.

In the night, the colors dance,
Inviting all to take a chance.
In echoes, we hear the call,
Through art, we rise, we never fall.

Colors of Compassion

Beneath the skies, a palette bright,
Comes forth the colors of pure light.
Each shade a hug, a tender care,
In unity, our hearts we share.

Red for love that fiercely glows,
Green for peace that gently flows.
Blue for trust, both deep and wide,
Together, we stand side by side.

Yellows weave through joy and grace,
While purples bring a warm embrace.
With every hue, let kindness grow,
In compassion's garden, life will flow.

In each heartbeat, colors blend,
A tapestry that knows no end.
Together painted, hand in hand,
In shades of love, together stand.

A Canvas of Companionship

In the quiet corners, laughter glows,
Brush strokes of friendship, love overflows.
Together we paint our dreams in light,
Colors entwined, hearts take flight.

Through valleys of doubt, we hold each hand,
With whispers of solace, we make a stand.
Every shared secret, a shade of trust,
In this vibrant bond, we flourish, we must.

Time holds no sway in our trusting embrace,
With every canvas, we find our place.
A masterpiece woven in warmth and care,
Where each little moment is precious and rare.

Rhapsody of Relaxation

In the gentle sway of twilight's glow,
Soft murmurs of peace begin to flow.
A serenade sung by the rustling leaves,
In this calm cocoon, the spirit believes.

With each passing hour, the world fades away,
In tranquil embrace, we choose to stay.
Melodies drift like clouds in the sky,
In rhapsody's arms, we're free to fly.

Crickets join in, a night-time choir,
As stars twinkle bright, our hearts grow higher.
A soothing lullaby wraps round the night,
In this tranquil realm, everything feels right.

The Soothing Spectrum

A canvas of hues, bright and divine,
Each color a whisper, a soft, gentle sign.
In sapphire dreams, the tides start to sway,
While golden dawn breaks, chasing shadows away.

Emerald laughter in the heart of the trees,
Where ruby sunsets dance with the breeze.
A symphony painted in strokes so light,
In this soothing spectrum, we find our light.

Life's vibrant shades blend in perfect grace,
A gallery of moments, a warm embrace.
With every heartbeat, a brush of the soul,
In this kaleidoscope, we become whole.

Palette of the Mind

In the quiet recesses where stories dwell,
Thoughts are the pigments, a vibrant spell.
Imaginations dance upon the canvas,
Where visions emerge, boundless and vast.

Each dream a color, vivid and bright,
Painting the shadows with strokes of light.
In the labyrinth of thoughts, creativity flows,
With every stroke, the inner child grows.

In a palette where fears and hopes collide,
A tapestry woven with time as our guide.
Here we explore, with passion and grace,
Crafting our journey, our own sacred space.

Meditative Murals

Colors swirl in silent grace,
Each stroke a calming space.
Whispers dance on painted walls,
Echoes of the heart's soft calls.

Gentle shadows intertwine,
Crafting peace, a sacred sign.
As the hues begin to fade,
Stillness in this art is made.

A canvas of the mind's own song,
Guiding where the thoughts belong.
In the stillness, beauty grows,
Meditative, where stillness flows.

Brushes dipped in quiet prayer,
Creating worlds beyond compare.
Art unfolds like morning light,
In this mural, pure delight.

Tones of Tranquil Thoughts

Softly hum the colors bright,
In each tone, a soul's delight.
Layers mix, a gentle blend,
Tranquil thoughts that never end.

Each shade a whispered plea,
Inviting peace to set us free.
Harmony in every hue,
Painting worlds where dreams come true.

Quiet moments linger long,
In these tones, we find our song.
Meditations weave through air,
Carved from dreams, with tender care.

Let the softest colors speak,
Calm and gentle, strong yet meek.
In the silence, thoughts take flight,
Amidst the tones, we find the light.

The Lullaby of Light

Light cascades in tender streams,
Filling hearts with gentle dreams.
Lullabies that softly glow,
Guiding hearts where hope can flow.

Golden rays and silver sighs,
Painting calm across the skies.
Each beam a sweet refrain sung,
In the night, where hope is strung.

Through the shadows, light will weave,
A gentle touch, we can believe.
Soft as whispers in the night,
In this dance, we find our flight.

Every flicker tells a tale,
In this warmth, we will not fail.
Cradling souls with every spark,
Lullabies that light the dark.

Harmonious Hues

Brushes stoke the vibrant fire,
Creating balance, pure desire.
Colors blend like joy and peace,
In this art, our worries cease.

Notes of azure, hints of gold,
Stories in the hues unfold.
Every tone a song so sweet,
Harmony beneath our feet.

The canvas sings in perfect tune,
Underneath the watchful moon.
Nature's palette finds its way,
In this dance, we wish to stay.

Each hue a heartbeat, rich and loud,
Together wrapped in color's shroud.
In these shades, our spirits rise,
Harmonious hues beneath the skies.

Shades of Solace

In whispers soft, the shadows fall,
Embracing peace, they gently call.
Each hue a story, each pause a breath,
In quiet corners, we find our rest.

Through twilight's veil, our worries fade,
In twilight's glow, new hopes cascade.
Colors blend in harmony's grace,
A tender moment, a sacred space.

With every stroke, a memory wakes,
In strokes of love, our spirit makes.
The palette speaks of days long gone,
Yet in its warmth, we're never alone.

A Symphony in Color

Notes of crimson dance with blue,
A melody crafted anew.
Each shade a song, each tint a rhyme,
In canvas dreams, we lose all time.

A crescendo's rise in emerald green,
A harmony felt, yet seldom seen.
With golden hues, the day ignites,
In twilight's calm, the symphony ignites.

Soft whispers of lavender grace,
In every corner, love finds its place.
An opus weaves through the air,
In each hue, a story to share.

The Calm Canvas

Upon the cloth, the stillness grows,
Where silence speaks, the heart just knows.
With gentle strokes, the colors blend,
A tranquil place where worries end.

Beneath the clouds of softest white,
The canvas holds both day and night.
In quiet hues, serenity lies,
A world reborn beneath soft skies.

Each brush a whisper, each shade a prayer,
In stillness found, we shed our care.
A gentle hand, a steady heart,
From chaos born, we find our art.

Reflections in Acrylic

In layers thick, the memories play,
Reflected light from yesterday.
Each drop a moment, each line a trace,
In shiny swirls, we find our place.

A dance of colors, bold and bright,
In reflections cast, we find our light.
A canvas speaks of love and fear,
In acrylic dreams, we find what's dear.

With every shimmer, stories flow,
In vibrant shades, our hearts we show.
The past resounds, the future calls,
In the artwork's grace, our spirit sprawls.

Colors of Compassion

In shades of red, a heart beats warm,
A gentle touch, a calming balm.
Soft blues wash over, love's embrace,
Together we find our rightful place.

Golden yellows, a brightened dawn,
Hope and kindness gently spawn.
Greens of nature, fresh and bright,
We nurture souls in fading light.

Violet whispers in twilight's glow,
Compassion blooms, and kindness flows.
Each color mingles, hand in hand,
Creating a world where we all stand.

Through every hue, our spirits rise,
In unity, we touch the skies.
Colors of compassion ever blend,
A masterpiece where hearts can mend.

A Symphony in Shades

A symphony of colors plays,
In vibrant notes through endless days.
Crimson flares like passion's fire,
While azure tunes lift hearts higher.

Emerald greens, a soothing sound,
Nature's chorus all around.
Golden glow sings warmth's refrain,
In every stroke, love's sweet gain.

Soft pastels in twilight's kiss,
Blend harmonies of tranquil bliss.
This canvas dances, paints the air,
With every color, joy to share.

A symphony, each hue a note,
In life's grand song, we all float.
Together we weave this bright tale,
A union of shades that will not fail.

Dreamlike Serenity

In quiet spaces, colors blend,
A dreamlike hue, where time can bend.
Soft lilacs whisper in the breeze,
While muted grays put hearts at ease.

Gentle aquas, serene and still,
Invite the mind to pause and chill.
Golden hour, a fleeting glow,
Beneath its charm, our troubles go.

In blushing pinks, the dawn awakes,
With every breath, a moment takes.
The canvas flows, both light and deep,
In dreamlike worlds, our souls can leap.

Serenity wraps in tender hue,
A tranquil space for me and you.
Through every shade, a calm retreat,
In colors soft, our spirits meet.

The Color of Rest

In muted tones, the day unwinds,
A soothing balm for weary minds.
Soft beige blankets, warm and light,
Embrace the night in sweet delight.

Gentle greys settle like the mist,
Quieting thoughts, like a tender kiss.
Dusk's deep blue, a curtain drawn,
Inviting dreams until the dawn.

A splash of indigo, calm and deep,
Calls us gently into sleep.
Lavender whispers, dreams take flight,
In colors soft, we find the night.

The color of rest, a sacred space,
Where peace and stillness find their place.
Together we breathe, as shadows cast,
In the color of rest, our worries pass.

Calmness in Color

Gentle hues of soft blue,
Whispers of the morning dew.
Painted skies in warm embrace,
Nature's breath, a calming space.

Fields of green, a tranquil sight,
Shimmering under golden light.
A palette rich with every shade,
In stillness, all worries fade.

Echoes of the quiet breeze,
Dancing through the swaying trees.
Each color sings a peaceful song,
In this realm, we all belong.

Harmony in every glance,
In colors, nature's sweet romance.
Calmness wrapped in vibrant art,
Healing whispers to the heart.

Canvas of Quietude

Blank canvas in the morning light,
A promise of peace, soft and bright.
Brush in hand, the world at bay,
Creating calm in hues of gray.

Each stroke a gentle lullaby,
Filling spaces, low and high.
Flowing lines, surrender's grace,
In quietude, we find our place.

Colors blend as dreams unfold,
Stories of the heart retold.
In silence, beauty starts to thrive,
On this canvas, we come alive.

Breath by breath, we watch and weave,
A tapestry that we believe.
Every shade a step toward peace,
In quietude, our worries cease.

Serenity's Masterpiece

In the stillness, whispers flow,
Nature's art, a tranquil show.
Mountains rise in quiet might,
Guardians of the soft twilight.

Reflecting ponds of crystal clear,
Mirroring all we hold dear.
Each ripple tells a tale of calm,
A soothing touch, a healing balm.

Underneath the ancient trees,
Rustling leaves sing melodies.
Forever captured in this space,
Serenity's gentle embrace.

A masterpiece of peace defined,
Each moment cherished, intertwined.
In nature's hush, we find our song,
Carried forth where we belong.

Spirit of Stillness

In the hush of dawn's first light,
Stillness holds the world in sight.
Every heartbeat, calm and clear,
Spirit of stillness, drawing near.

Softly echoes through the trees,
Breezes weave, a gentle tease.
In this peace, the mind can roam,
Finding solace, feeling home.

Moments drift like clouds above,
Wrapped in warmth, in quiet love.
The spirit whispers through the air,
A promise found, beyond compare.

In the calm, we come alive,
In stillness, dreams begin to thrive.
Every breath a step, a chance,
To embrace the world's sweet dance.

Flickering Patches of Calm

In the quiet of the night,
Stars whisper soft and bright.
Moonlight dances on the leaves,
A gentle breeze, the heart believes.

Rippling water, glinting light,
Reflections of a cozy sight.
Nature hums a soothing tune,
As shadows play beneath the moon.

Whispers carried through the air,
Sparks of joy not meant to share.
In this moment, still and clear,
The world seems calm, free from fear.

In patches flicker peace anew,
Wrapped in night's deep velvet hue.
We breathe in and then we sigh,
Embraced by calm as time slips by.

Tints of Togetherness

Hand in hand, we wander wide,
Amidst the hues, hearts open wide.
Every laughter sings a song,
Creating bonds where we belong.

In gardens bloom, our colors blend,
Each moment shared, a precious friend.
Sunset paints the sky in pink,
With every touch, we learn to think.

Waves crash down, we stand as one,
Under the warmth of setting sun.
Side by side through thick and thin,
With every loss, we find a win.

From tints of joy to deepest sorrow,
Together, we'll meet each tomorrow.
In every shade, we find our way,
A brighter dawn for us to play.

Harmonized Horizons

Past the mountains, skies will blend,
Where sun and moon, as lovers, send.
Colors mingle in warm embrace,
A cosmic dance, a timed grace.

Echoes of a distant chime,
Flowing freely, unbound by time.
Together, we can touch the high,
Where earth meets with the open sky.

Underneath the vast expanse,
Life takes on a gentle chance.
With every heartbeat, dreams unfold,
In harmonies both soft and bold.

Horizons call, they pull us near,
In every whisper, love sincere.
We rise together, hand in hand,
With faith and hope, a destined land.

Serenity in Shades

In twilight's glow, peace softly spreads,
As daylight fades, the night thread.
Whispers linger, colors fade,
Moments cherished, never weighed.

Gentle clouds drift in the breeze,
Carried softly like secrets' tease.
Underneath the endless sky,
Serenity teaches us to fly.

Every shade tells a story true,
In muted tones, the heart renews.
Nature cradles all our fears,
As tranquility draws us near.

In shadows deep, we find our place,
A quiet refuge, warm embrace.
Within the softest, shaded glade,
Serenity sings, and fears evade.

Serenity's Palette

Soft hues blend in quiet grace,
Whispers of peace in every space.
Gentle strokes of blue and green,
Nature's calm, a soothing scene.

A canvas vast, where dreams take flight,
In twilight's glow, the world feels right.
Golden rays of sun descend,
In twilight's arms, all sorrows mend.

Fragrant blooms in colors bright,
Butterflies dance in golden light.
Each petal tells a story bold,
Of love, of life, forever told.

In stillness found, our hearts embrace,
This quiet place, our resting space.
With every hue, our spirits soar,
In serenity, we seek for more.

Where Colors Meet Silence

Amidst the hush, the colors play,
In silence wrapped, they gently sway.
A tapestry of hues aligned,
Where quiet moments are refined.

Reds like fire, deep and true,
Soft pastels, a tranquil view.
On canvas blank, emotions blend,
In colors bright, the heart can mend.

Whispers drift on gentle breeze,
Carried forth with perfect ease.
In every shade, a story spun,
Where colors meet, two hearts are one.

In the stillness, we can hear,
The silent song that draws us near.
A dance of hues, a painter's grace,
In this serene and sacred space.

Dreamscapes in Pastels

In twilight's glow, dreams softly weave,
Pastel clouds, a place to believe.
Cotton candy skies up high,
Whispers of wishes as time slips by.

A gentle breeze through fields of cream,
Floating softly on a shimmering stream.
Petals blush in rosy light,
Where dreams awaken in the night.

Laughter dances on the air,
Every color sings a prayer.
In the quiet, hearts unite,
Under stars that twinkle bright.

Here in hues, our visions swirl,
A painted path in a vibrant whirl.
In pastel dreams, we find our way,
To tomorrow's dawn from yesterday.

The Gentle Brush

With every stroke, the canvas sighs,
Colors bloom beneath the skies.
A gentle brush, like whispers play,
Crafting moments as dreams sway.

In shades of hope, we paint anew,
Each dot of light, a love so true.
The curves of life, soft and kind,
Reflections of what love can find.

A dance of hues upon the page,
In stillness found, we disengage.
The quiet art of hearts laid bare,
In every line, a tender care.

As twilight falls, we share our grace,
In this soft moment, we find our place.
With gentle brush, our spirits shine,
In colors blended, your heart with mine.

The Serenity Spectrum

From azure skies to golden seas,
A gentle breeze that flows with ease.
Each hue a whisper, soft and light,
Inviting calm, a pure delight.

In shades of green, the heart will rest,
Nature's palette, truly blessed.
Lavender dreams in twilight's grace,
Time suspended, a warm embrace.

Violet hues at day's farewell,
In quiet tones, our thoughts can dwell.
With every shade, a story shared,
In silence felt, in peace declared.

Embrace the spectrum, wide and vast,
In every moment, hold it fast.
For in serenity's gentle land,
We find our peace, a guiding hand.

Mellow Moments in Color

Soft peach dawns and sunset sighs,
Whispers of warmth beneath clear skies.
Gentle pastels, hues of grace,
Life's tender touch in every space.

Muted golds and lilac trails,
Carry the heart where comfort prevails.
In slow, sweet rhythms, time will flow,
Painting the world in a subtle glow.

Turquoise laughs and coral dreams,
In every shade, a comfort beams.
Mellow moments, softly spun,
A tapestry of warmth and fun.

In vivid strokes of love and light,
We cherish joy, we cherish bright.
The colors blend, a life embraced,
In mellow moments, time is traced.

Brush of Breath

A stroke of air, the sigh of dawn,
Where quiet whispers gently yawn.
With every breath, a canvas forms,
The brush of life, through peace it warms.

Fleeting shadows, soft and fleet,
Dance on the ground where spirits meet.
Each pulse a color, rich and wide,
An artist's heart, a soothing tide.

With vibrant thoughts, we paint the skies,
In every heart, a dream that flies.
In every brush of breath, we see,
The art of life, wild and free.

As seasons change, the strokes evolve,
In harmony, life's truth we solve.
With each exhale, a story told,
In every breath, a promise bold.

The Quiet Expanse

In the quiet expanse of starlit night,
Reflections shimmer, pure and bright.
The world a whisper, soft and deep,
In this space, our souls can leap.

Endless skies, where silence sings,
A tranquil peace that freedom brings.
Underneath the cosmic canvas wide,
We find our dreams, our hearts collide.

With gentle shadows, thoughts take wing,
In solitude, the mind will cling.
To moments still, where time is free,
The quiet expanse, our sanctuary.

And as the dawn begins to wake,
The stillness holds what dreams can make.
In the quiet, hearts expand,
With every breath, together we stand.

Echoes of Ease

In the calm of dawn's first light,
Whispers dance in gentle flight.
Hearts unburdened, spirits soar,
In the stillness, we explore.

Nature breathes a sigh of peace,
As worries fade and troubles cease.
Time slows down, each moment's clear,
In echoes soft, we draw near.

Breezes carry sweet refrain,
Lifting shadows, easing pain.
Together, we find our way,
In the hush of a perfect day.

With every heartbeat, true release,
In the echoes, find your ease.
Let the world whisper and tease,
In the melody of peace.

The Peaceful Easel

Upon the canvas, colors flow,
Strokes of harmony start to grow.
With every hue, the heart reveals,
A world where every soul can heal.

The brush reveals a tranquil scene,
Nature's touch, a vibrant green.
With every line, tension unwinds,
In art's embrace, pure thought finds.

Sunset glows in orange and gold,
Stories of warmth and love unfold.
In this space where spirits twine,
Peaceful visions intertwine.

Each layer whispers soft and sweet,
A dance of colors at our feet.
On this easel, dreams decrease,
A sanctuary, a sense of peace.

Soft Shades of Surrender

In twilight hues, we softly fade,
A gentle promise, love conveyed.
Each shade a sigh, a sweet release,
In soft surrender, find your peace.

The sky, a blanket, cool and wide,
Embraces all, with arms open wide.
Stars emerge, a twinkling song,
In this stillness, we belong.

Moonlight drapes the earth in grace,
Quiet pauses fill the space.
With every breath, let tension go,
In soft shades, feel the glow.

As nature whispers to the night,
We find ourselves in soft delight.
Let every worry drift away,
In surrender, we will stay.

Illusions of Inner Quiet

In the silence, echoes play,
Fleeting dreams drift far away.
Thoughts collide in shadowed streams,
A tapestry of whispered dreams.

Beneath the noise, a hidden calm,
A gentle pulse, a healing balm.
Illusions shatter, light breaks through,
In inner peace, find something new.

Waves of stillness wash the shore,
Cleansing hearts forevermore.
With every breath, the layers peel,
To reveal truths we can feel.

In this stillness, we confide,
As the chaos turns to tide.
Illusions fade, yet we ignite,
In the glow of inner light.

Dreams in Watercolor

In hues of blue, we softly drift,
A canvas wide, where hopes are lifted.
With brush of light, each moment gleams,
We paint our lives with vibrant dreams.

The swirls of pink and golden rays,
Illuminate our quiet days.
In every stroke, a story flows,
In watercolor, our essence shows.

As clouds of lavender float by,
Our wishes dance beneath the sky.
Each drop a memory, pure and bright,
Transforming shadows into light.

Together in this art we make,
With every shade, we gently wake.
In dreams of watercolor we find,
A world of wonder, intertwined.

Essence of Ease

Beneath the shade of willow trees,
A whispering breeze sings songs of ease.
The day unfolds, serene and light,
As hours stretch softly into night.

Gentle laughter fills the air,
With joyous hearts, we have a care.
In hidden glades, our spirits soar,
The essence of ease forevermore.

Moments linger like the dew,
With tender thoughts and skies of blue.
In this tranquil space we find,
A rhythm sweet, in heart and mind.

The world slows down, our worries cease,
In every breath, we find our peace.
The simple joys, they hold the key,
To live within this essence of ease.

The Serene Spectrum

A rainbow arches through the sky,
In colors bright, they burst and fly.
Each shade a tale of love and grace,
In the serene spectrum, we find our place.

Halos of gold in morning's light,
Guide wandering souls into the bright.
In violets soft, our hearts align,
Finding harmony in every line.

The ocean's blue, a soothing balm,
Where chaos fades and spirits calms.
With every hue, a chance to grow,
In the spectrum's dance, our feelings flow.

As night unfolds in shades of grey,
The stars remind us, we're here to stay.
In this serene embrace, we trust,
To color our dreams in love and lust.

Merging Melodies of Color

In the symphony of sunset's eye,
Colors harmonize, the day whispers goodbye.
With every brushstroke, music plays,
Merging melodies of vibrant arrays.

The notes of red, like hearts aflame,
Resonate softly, calling our name.
Blues that echo through the serene,
Compose a tune of peace unseen.

In the twilight's glow, we find our song,
A palette of hues where we belong.
The lively beats of yellow and green,
Intertwining in a dance divine, unseen.

As night descends and shadows blend,
The music lingers, it knows no end.
In merging melodies, we create,
A canvas of life, we celebrate.

Serenity's Strokes

Whispers of the morning light,
Gentle breezes, pure delight.
Cascading waves kiss the shore,
In their rhythm, we explore.

Clouds drift softly, shadows play,
Nature's canvas, bright and gay.
Colors blend in perfect grace,
In this haven, find your place.

Silence speaks in soothing tones,
Heartfelt magic, no more moans.
Every brushstroke, calm and slow,
Guides our souls where peace can grow.

Let the world fade from your mind,
In this stillness, strength you'll find.
Serenity paints life anew,
In its hues, we start to bloom.

Portraits of Peace

In the twilight's soft embrace,
Echoes of a quiet space.
Golden suns dip into night,
Painting dreams with tender light.

Mountains rise, tall and proud,
Wrapped in a soft, gentle shroud.
Fragrant blooms in gardens bloom,
Filling hearts with sweet perfume.

Stars appear, sparking the sky,
Flickering lights, they seem to sigh.
Nature whispers, beckons near,
In its presence, hold no fear.

Canvas of a tranquil mind,
Life's true essence we will find.
Every stroke a tale to tell,
In this peace, we know so well.

The Gentle Canvas

Brushes dance with colors bright,
Creating visions, pure delight.
A whisper here, a touch of blue,
Breath of nature, bold and true.

Sunrise paints the morning gold,
Stories of a day unfold.
Every hue, a gentle sigh,
Underneath the vast, wide sky.

Rippling streams reflect the trees,
Carrying peace upon the breeze.
Clouds drift softly, dreams awake,
In their arms, our hearts won't ache.

In this art, we find a way,
To embrace both night and day.
On this canvas, lives are spun,
In the quiet, we are one.

Vivid Visions of Calm

Dancing leaves with stories told,
Echoes of a world so bold.
In the silence, moments last,
Painting futures, bright and vast.

Rippling waters, crystal clear,
Carving paths that draw us near.
As the moonlight gently glows,
Life's true beauty softly shows.

Gentle waves upon the shore,
Whisper secrets, want for more.
In the twilight, dreams take flight,
Guided by the stars at night.

Canvas filled with joy and peace,
In this stillness, heart's release.
Vivid brushes, love's sweet balm,
In this space, we find our calm.

Palette of Harmony

In shades of blue, the sky does sing,
A gentle blend, a soothing thing.
The sun dips low, its golden touch,
Brings warmth and peace, it means so much.

With splashes bright, the flowers bloom,
Their hues dispel the winter's gloom.
In every petal, life does hum,
A canvas rich, where dreams do come.

The whispering winds, they softly call,
Their melody, a sweet enthrall.
With every stroke, and every hue,
In harmony, we find what's true.

Together here, in joyful dance,
We paint the world, embrace the chance.
With laughter shared and hands entwined,
A palette bright, our hearts aligned.

Stillness in the Spectrum

A quiet dusk with colors soft,
Where echoes fade and spirits loft.
The gentle brush of twilight's hand,
In silence, dreams begin to stand.

Each shade employed, a whisper sweet,
In nature's glow, our hearts entreat.
A canvas built of stillness rare,
In every hue, a tranquil prayer.

The stars ignite, a twinkling show,
In night's embrace, our worries slow.
A spectrum wide, yet finely tuned,
In stillness found, our souls are hewn.

Embrace the calm, let fears subside,
In nature's arms, we'll take our stride.
For in the peace of twilight's call,
We find our place, we find it all.

Mellow Tides

The waves caress the sandy shore,
A rhythm soft, forevermore.
In shades of teal and azure bright,
They dance with grace beneath the light.

The sun dips low, the sky aglow,
With colors rich, a soft tableau.
A tranquil sea, both vast and wide,
Invites the soul to drift and glide.

The whispers of the ocean's flow,
Bring secrets deep where currents go.
With every ebb and every swell,
A story waits, a silent spell.

Embrace the calm, let worries fade,
In mellow tides, we find our shade.
Together here, where silence reigns,
We sail through life, release our chains.

Brushstrokes of Solitude

In solitude, the colors blend,
A quiet place where moments mend.
Each brushstroke tells a tale untold,
In deepened hues, the heart unfolds.

Whispers soft in twilight's glow,
Where shadows stretch and feelings flow.
The canvas blank, yet rich inside,
In solitude, our thoughts collide.

With every stroke, the silence grows,
As depth and light, together flows.
A world apart, yet deeply known,
In brushstrokes' dance, we find our own.

In quietude, the spirit sighs,
With every shade, the self defies.
An artist's heart, in solitude,
Creates a love that's pure and good.

Palette of Promises

Whispers of hope in brush strokes bright,
A canvas awaits, chasing the night.
Each hue a wish, each shade a dream,
In a world reborn, love's gentle gleam.

With every mix, life's stories unfold,
Moments of warmth, tales softly told.
From dawn to dusk, colors entwine,
In this palette, our spirits align.

Mosaics of Comfort

Pieces of life scattered wide,
Together they form, a warm guide.
Fragments of laughter, moments shared,
In this mosaic, love is declared.

Each tile a memory, polished and bright,
Reflecting the beauty, cradling the light.
A sanctuary built, one bit at a time,
In the heart's embrace, we forever climb.

The Colors of Contentment

Gentle hues of amber and gold,
Wrap me in warmth, a soft hold.
A canvas where peace starts to blend,
In silent moments, hearts can mend.

The blues bring solace, the greens bring life,
Amidst the chaos, far from strife.
Every stroke whispers, "Here, just be,"
In the colors around, I find me.

Tapestry of Restfulness

Threads of tranquility weave through the night,
Soft whispers of dreams span left and right.
Each stitch a moment, a breath held tight,
In this tapestry, everything feels right.

Patterns of peace in shades so calm,
Embracing the soul with a soothing balm.
Knotted in comfort, securely bound,
In the soft fabric, true solace found.

Radiant Refuge

In the quiet glen, light spills,
Where shadows dance and time stands still.
Beneath the boughs of ancient trees,
A gentle breeze carries the pleas.

Soft whispers call from distant hills,
As the heart with peace gently fills.
A haven where the soul can soar,
In this embrace, we need no more.

The sun dips low with golden grace,
Illuminating this sacred space.
Here, worries fade like morning mist,
In radiant refuge, love exists.

With every sunset's warm embrace,
We find our place, we find our pace.
A tapestry of dreams unfold,
In this refuge, bright and bold.

The Harmony of Shades

Colors blend in soft embrace,
A symphony of light's sweet face.
Underneath the twilight's glow,
Subtle hues begin to flow.

Violet whispers greet the night,
While stars awake to share their light.
Each shade a note in night's grand song,
In harmony, where we belong.

The canvas draped with colors bright,
Paints a world of pure delight.
In tranquil tones, our spirits rise,
With every brush, a dream that flies.

Where shadows meet with dawn's first gleam,
We find the path, we dare to dream.
In this dance of dark and bright,
The harmony of shades takes flight.

Tranquility's Canvas

The pond reflects the sky's deep blue,
A perfect world for me and you.
With every ripple, peace flows near,
In tranquility, all is clear.

Soft petals drift on gentle air,
Nature's art, so rich and rare.
Where silence speaks in soothing tones,
We find our hearts, we find our homes.

The brush of dusk paints soft the hills,
As daylight's magic gently spills.
In every corner, beauty's found,
A canvas where our souls are bound.

With every breath, we take our time,
In tranquil moments, life's pure rhyme.
In this embrace, our worries cease,
Tranquility's canvas brings us peace.

Brush of Whispering Winds

The winds whisper secrets of the day,
Carrying dreams, they drift away.
Through the branches, their song resounds,
In nature's arms, magic abounds.

They dance with leaves, a gentle sway,
In twilight's glow, they softly play.
Each gust a tale from lands afar,
Guiding hearts like a wandering star.

With every breeze, a warm caress,
A promise of calm, a sweet redress.
In silence, they weave through the trees,
A tapestry of memories.

The brush of winds through fields so wide,
Invites us forth, a joyful ride.
In the whispers, we find our song,
With nature's breath, we all belong.

The Art of Quietude

In the hush of dawn's first light,
Whispers dance in soft delight.
Stillness paints the waking sky,
Beneath the calm, the worries sigh.

Moments linger, gently held,
In silence, secrets are revealed.
The heart beats slow, the mind at ease,
In quietude, we find our peace.

Time drifts like leaves on a stream,
Carrying hopes, carrying dreams.
The world outside, a distant sound,
In stillness, our true selves are found.

Breathe in deep the tranquil air,
Each exhale sheds the weight of care.
Embrace the calm, let go of race,
In quietude, find your space.

Chromatic Refuge

In hues of red and shades of blue,
Colors blend as dreams come true.
A canvas wide, an open heart,
Each stroke a wish, each shade a part.

Greens awaken the sleeping soul,
Yellows shine, making us whole.
In this refuge, we explore,
The vibrant paths to evermore.

Patterns swirl, a dance of light,
Creating joy in every sight.
Every color tells a tale,
Of journeys long, of winds that sail.

In chromatic waves, we find our place,
Wrapped in warmth, in sweet embrace.
With every hue, our spirits sing,
Within this realm, we feel the spring.

Nature's Gentle Embrace

Underneath the ancient trees,
Softly rustling in the breeze.
Nature holds us in her sway,
Guiding us through light and gray.

Petals fall like whispered dreams,
Crystal streams with gentle beams.
In every leaf and every stone,
We find a space we can call home.

Mountains rise to greet the sky,
Where eagles soar and loons cry.
With every step on earthy ground,
In nature's arms, our peace is found.

Wrapped in warmth of sun and shade,
In her presence, fears do fade.
Nature's love, a sweet embrace,
A canvas vast, a sacred space.

Spectrum of Stillness

In twilight's grasp, the colors blend,
A quiet call that seems to send.
Across the sky, a gentle sweep,
Where echoes of the day now sleep.

Night's embrace, so soft and wide,
In stillness, dreams begin to glide.
Stars twinkle in the silent dark,
Each a wish, a hopeful spark.

Shadows linger, softly fall,
Whispers float, like a muted call.
In every pause, in every sigh,
The world shrinks down, and we reach high.

This spectrum deep, of calm and grace,
Invites us to a sacred space.
With every breath, we come alive,
In stillness, restless hearts revive.

Solace in Every Stroke

In every stroke, a peace unfolds,
Calming colors, tales retold.
A quiet mind begins to glow,
In the stillness, feelings flow.

Brush in hand, I find my ground,
Whispers of solace all around.
Each hue's embrace, a soft caress,
In art, I find my happiness.

The canvas sings, a gentle tune,
Beneath the light of a silver moon.
A world created through my heart,
In every stroke, I find my art.

With every line, a breath, a sigh,
As colors dance and shadows lie.
Solace waits in each pure dream,
Embraced within the painter's theme.

Harmony's Brush

With harmony's brush, the world takes flight,
Colors mingle, pure delight.
Each shade a whisper, soft and true,
A soothing balm, in every hue.

In spirals of laughter, the canvas sways,
As light and shadow intertwine in plays.
Artistry flows like a gentle stream,
Crafting a land where moments dream.

A palette rich, a vibrant blend,
Each stroke composing, mend to mend.
In every crease, a story grows,
In harmony, the heart bestows.

Creativity bursts, a joyful flood,
Painting peace within the mud.
With harmony's brush, I find my way,
In every instance, a brighter day.

Whispers of Serenity

In whispers soft, the colors sway,
Painting peace in the light of day.
Moments captured in gentle strokes,
Where silence sings and the heart invokes.

Each brush connects a tale so vast,
A canvas living, holding fast.
In gradients of calm, I find my voice,
Each line a choice, a soft rejoice.

In tranquil shades, the world anew,
With every stroke, my spirit flew.
Whispers of serenity guide my hand,
Creating visions, quiet and grand.

Through artful means, I weave my soul,
Finding comfort in every goal.
In the stillness, I taste the grace,
Whispers echo in this sacred space.

Canvas of Calm

Upon this canvas, calm does bloom,
Colors whisper in every room.
Brush strokes trace a tranquil path,
Inviting peace, a gentle bath.

Moments linger in hues divine,
A dance of shadow and light align.
In stillness found, emotions play,
As colors breathe and drift away.

Canvas of calm, a serene embrace,
Art transforms this sacred space.
With every touch, the worries cease,
In painted realms, I find my peace.

The world outside fades far from view,
In strokes of solace, I start anew.
Each line a whisper of soft refrain,
The canvas holds a soothing gain.

Tranquil Tints

Soft whispers in the sky,
Pastels blend and gently sigh,
The world slows its hurried pace,
In hues of calm, we find our place.

Morning light on waking leaves,
Gentle brushstrokes weave and cleave,
Nature's lullaby unfolds,
In tranquil tints, serenity molds.

The river glimmers, blue and green,
In the silence, peace is seen,
Cotton clouds drift slowly by,
Underneath the painted sky.

As twilight wraps the day in grace,
Softening shadows start to trace,
A canvas vast, the stars ignite,
In tranquil tints, we find our light.

The Warm Embrace of Color

Golden rays of sunlight fall,
Warmth and brightness, nature's call,
Crimson blossoms kiss the air,
In every hue, love's gentle care.

Amber fields sway in the breeze,
Painted sunsets, hearts at ease,
Lavender whispers dusk's sweet song,
In colors bold, we all belong.

The twinkling stars, a velvet night,
Canopies of joy and light,
A warm embrace in every shade,
In this palette, dreams are laid.

With every stroke, the world ignites,
The warm embrace of color delights,
In splashes bright, we find our way,
As love and beauty gently play.

Emblems of Ease

Lush green leaves underfoot lie,
Whispers carried on the sigh,
Petals drift like soft confetti,
Emblems of ease, light and petty.

A gentle breeze rolls through the trees,
Nature's laughter on the leaves,
Sun-kissed paths where shadows dance,
In this moment, we take a chance.

Birds in flight, a joyous spree,
The world unfolds in harmony,
With every breath, we find release,
In simple joys, our hearts increase.

Together in this soft embrace,
We chase the tranquil, tender grace,
Emblems of ease, forever dear,
In every smile, love draws near.

Dappled Dreams

Sunlight filters through the leaves,
Where the heart learns and believes,
Patterns dance upon the ground,
In dappled dreams, hope is found.

Fluttering wings of bright butterflies,
Whispered secrets as time flies,
The world shifts in gentle streams,
Painting life in dappled dreams.

Winding paths, a hidden way,
Where shadows mingle with the day,
Each moment wrapped in softest beams,
A tapestry of dappled dreams.

In these spaces, we unwind,
Nature's canvas, pure and kind,
With every step, the magic seems,
To lead us home through dappled dreams.

Canvas of Calm

A gentle breeze stirs the air,
Brushes dipped in peace and care.
Colors blend, soft and warm,
Creating beauty, free from harm.

In twilight's glow, the shadows play,
As night unfolds, it drifts away.
Stars join in a silent waltz,
The canvas breathes, no need for faults.

Ripples dance on the water's face,
Reflecting the hues of nature's grace.
Every stroke sings a quiet song,
In this haven, we all belong.

So linger here, in twilight's scene,
Where calm resides and hearts feel keen.
A masterpiece, the world so bright,
In this canvas, find your light.

Tranquil Hues

Soft lilacs whisper in the breeze,
Petals unfurl with effortless ease.
The sun dips low, a golden ray,
Painting skies in games of play.

Emerald leaves sway, gently dance,
Nature's rhythm, a sweet romance.
Birds sing low, a serenade,
In tranquil hues, our fears will fade.

A path of stones, where shadows lie,
Crickets hum beneath the sky.
Moments captured, fleeting time,
In tranquil hues, all feels sublime.

So breathe in deep, let worries cease,
In this palette, find your peace.
A world of color, rich and true,
Embraced within these tranquil hues.

Serenity Strokes

In quiet corners, secrets live,
Each brush reveals what hearts can give.
With shades of blue and whispers light,
Serenity glows in the soft twilight.

Mountains rise, their peaks aglow,
Reflecting dreams in the world below.
A gentle touch, the world anew,
In strokes of serenity, we renew.

Clouds drift lazily, a soft caress,
Nature's peace, our souls confess.
In every shade, a story told,
Serenity strokes, pure and bold.

Let go of worries, let the heart flow,
In this canvas, find warmth and glow.
A tranquil palette, life unfolds,
In serenity's grasp, we break the molds.

Whispers of Color

Across the fields, the poppies sway,
Whispers of color, bright and gay.
Each petal folds a tale of grace,
In nature's heart, we find our place.

Sketches of life, both soft and loud,
In each vibrant hue, we feel proud.
The sun paints gold on the daily grind,
Whispers of color, a love unconfined.

Through forests deep and rivers wide,
Colors call, and we abide.
In every step, let visions roam,
Whispers of color, our vibrant home.

So listen close to the earth's soft song,
In the tapestry of life, we all belong.
A world adorned, let dreams unfurl,
In the whispers of color, we embrace the swirl.

Echoes of a Colorful Dawn

The sun peeks shyly from the east,
Awakening dreams with gentle light.
Birds sing sweetly, nature's feast,
As shadows dance in morning's sight.

Whispers of dew on blades of grass,
Colors bloom in vibrant grace.
Time moves slowly, moments pass,
In this serene and sacred place.

The sky ablaze with orange hues,
Clouds painted in soft strokes of gold.
Each breath a gift, each sight a muse,
A symphony of warmth to behold.

Echoes linger in the air,
Life unfolds with every ray.
Hope and joy, beyond compare,
Welcome in the dawning day.

Tints of Tranquility

Soft blues whisper in the breeze,
A tranquil lake reflects the sky.
Gentle ripples, nature's tease,
Time stands still as moments fly.

Lilies float with graceful ease,
Petals blush in muted tones.
In this haven, hearts appease,
Listening to the nature's moans.

Mountains cradle silent dreams,
Veils of mist in quiet embrace.
Sunsets weave their golden seams,
Crafting peace in this sacred space.

With every breath, a soothing balm,
Colors blend in soft array.
Each heartbeat sings a timeless psalm,
In the stillness of the day.

Merging with the Palette

The artist dips the brush in bliss,
A canvas waits for dreams to blend.
Each stroke a wish, a painter's kiss,
Colors dance, as colors mend.

Reds and greens in harmony,
Swirls of purple, bursts of gold.
Merging souls in unity,
A story of creation told.

From chaos rises wonder's sight,
Shadows whisper tales of hue.
In the vibrant, shifting light,
Life's essence painted, ever true.

As colors mingle, hearts align,
Visions soar, and spirits play.
Art and life in pure design,
Creating beauty every day.

Silent Landscapes

In fields where quiet shadows grow,
Mountains stand like ancient guards.
The world moves slow, its heartbeats low,
Nature whispers soft regards.

Beneath the boughs of willow trees,
Creatures stir in gentle peace.
The air is sweet with fragrant breeze,
In stillness, all worries cease.

Golden fields stretch far away,
A canvas of the earth's embrace.
In silence, find the words to say,
To treasure time, a sacred space.

Each moment lingers, pure delight,
As twilight wraps the day in sighs.
In silent landscapes, hearts take flight,
Where beauty lives and never dies.

Milton Keynes UK
Ingram Content Group UK Ltd.
UKHW022118251124
451529UK00012B/586

9 789916 907030